Should Students Have to Take

TESTS?

By Robert M. Hamilton

KidHaven
PUBLISHING

Published in 2018 by
KidHaven Publishing, an Imprint of Greenhaven Publishing, LLC
353 3rd Avenue
Suite 255
New York, NY 10010

Designer: Seth Hughes
Editor: Katie Kawa

Photo credits: Cover dolgachov/iStock/Thinkstock; p. 5 (top) JGI/Jamie Grill/Blend Images/Getty Images; p. 5 (bottom) Syda Productions/Shutterstock.com; p. 7 Past Pix/SSPL/Getty Images; p. 9 © istockphoto.com/Wavebreakmedia; p. 11 Hemera Technologies/AbleStock.com/Thinkstock, p. 13 David Shopper/Corbis/Getty Images; p. 15 racorn/Shutterstock.com; p. 17 wavebreakmedia/ Shutterstock.com; p. 19 pyotr021/iStock/Thinkstock; p. 21 (notepad) ESB Professional/ Shutterstock.com; p. 21 (markers) Kucher Serhii/Shutterstock.com; p. 21 (photo frame) FARBAI/ iStock/Thinkstock; p. 21 (inset, left) Tanya Constantine/Blend Images/Thinkstock; p. 21 (inset, middle-left) Tim Boyle/Getty Images; p. 21 (inset, middle-right) Creatas/Creatas/Thinkstock; p. 21 (inset, right) Ingram Publishing/Thinkstock.

Cataloging-in-Publication Data

Names: Hamilton, Robert M.
Title: Should students have to take tests? / Robert M. Hamilton .
Description: New York : KidHaven Publishing, 2018. | Series: Points of view | Includes index.
Identifiers: ISBN 9781534523449 (pbk.) | 9781534523463 (library bound) | ISBN 9781534523456 (6 pack) | ISBN 9781534523470 (ebook)
Subjects: LCSH: Educational tests and measurements–United States–Juvenile literature.
Classification: LCC LB3051.H3455 2018 | DDC 371.26–dc23

Printed in the United States of America

CPSIA compliance information: Batch #BS17KL: For further information contact Greenhaven Publishing LLC, New York, New York at 1-844-317-7404.

Please visit our website, www.greenhavenpublishing.com. For a free color catalog of all our high-quality books, call toll free 1-844-317-7404 or fax 1-844-317-7405.

CONTENTS

The Great Testing
DEBATE

Tests are a common part of life for students, but are they necessary? Many people believe they are. They think tests are the best way to see how well students are learning what they're being taught and how well teachers are doing their jobs. Other people, however, believe tests are not the best way to show how smart students are.

A world without tests might be easier, but would it actually be better for students? Before you answer this question, it's helpful to understand the facts on both sides. This is called having an informed opinion.

Know the Facts!

Standardized tests are tests that are taken and graded in a consistent way. This allows graders to compare students based on how they do on the test.

People have different points of view about **issues** such as taking tests. It helps to understand these different points of view before deciding how you feel about an issue.

Testing Throughout
HISTORY

People have been taking tests to show how much they know since ancient times. In ancient China, people who wanted government jobs had to first pass a test. In the late 1800s, standardized tests became popular in the United States as a way to test the increasing number of students in American schools.

Today, students take many different kinds of tests. They take tests given by their teachers as well as standardized tests that are given to students across their state and the whole country. These kinds of tests have many supporters but also many opponents.

Know the Facts!

Standardized testing on the state level increased after the No Child Left Behind Act of 2001 was signed into law by President George W. Bush.

Taking tests has been a part of life for students for hundreds of years.

A Measuring TOOL

Throughout history, tests have been a kind of measuring tool. They measure how students are learning, and they also measure how teachers are teaching. People who support standardized tests see them as the best way to measure how well teachers are doing their jobs. Some schools use these tests as a way to decide if teachers can keep their jobs.

Teachers can use tests as a way to see if their teaching methods are working. If students are doing poorly on tests, teachers can change how they're presenting their lessons to help students understand things more clearly.

Know the Facts!

The U.S. government requires that all states test students on math, science, and reading.

Testing can be seen as a tool to help teachers become better at their jobs.

Teaching to
THE TEST

Some people think tests can be used to help teachers, but others think tests actually make teachers worse at their jobs. Parents, students, and teachers themselves often worry about "teaching to the test." This means that teachers become so **focused** on standardized tests that they only teach what's on those tests.

When teachers only teach to the test, students only learn certain lessons and skills. This can lead to boring classes and teachers under a lot of **stress**. People worry that teaching to the test keeps students from getting a well-rounded education.

Know the Facts!

In 2015, 20 percent of students in New York State opted out of, or chose not to take, state standardized tests. This was the highest percentage in the United States that year.

Some teachers believe standardized tests have changed how they teach, and they don't like teaching to the tests. They think it makes school less fun for teachers and students.

LEARN

Teaching to the test bothers some teachers. Other teachers, however, believe they can still do their jobs well and create fun classrooms while preparing students for tests.

Many teachers understand that tests can actually help students learn. **Frequent** testing has been proven to help students remember what they've been taught. It's also been proven to help students recall what they've learned more quickly than they would if they hadn't been tested on it. Tests serve as a way for students to find gaps in their understanding. Once they fill those gaps, they can do better on the next test.

Know the Facts!

Studies have shown that the best kind of testing to help students remember facts is frequent testing during a **unit** rather than at the end of it.

Tests are also a good way for parents to see how well their children are doing in school.

Test ANXIETY

Tests can help students see how well they're doing in class, but this isn't always a good thing. For some students, this creates a lot of stress because they want to do well. Tests can cause some students to lose sleep because they're studying for a long time or because they're afraid of doing poorly.

Test anxiety happens to some students. When someone has test anxiety, their body **responds** to the stress of taking a test. They might feel sick or feel like they're going to pass out.

Know the Facts!

Up to 20 percent of students in the United States have test anxiety, as stated by the American Test Anxieties Association.

If you think you have test anxiety, it's good to talk to your parents or teacher about it.

COMPARISONS

People who believe tests are important for students understand that tests can cause stress. However, they still believe tests are the best way to easily compare students within schools and across states.

Standardized tests are seen as a fair and objective, or fact-based, way for people to see how their class, school, school **district**, or state compares to others. In some cases, these comparisons lead to new programs, new teaching methods, or increases in **funding** for schools that need help raising their students' test scores.

Know the Facts!

Many standardized tests are graded by computers, which takes away the chance that they could be graded incorrectly because of **human error**.

Many people believe test scores are the only objective way to compare students.

Not Always
ACCURATE

Test scores might be an easy way to compare students, but some people have argued that they're not the most **accurate** way. They believe test scores aren't always a good way to measure how smart students are.

Tests don't take into account outside factors. For example, if a student is sick the day of a test, they might do poorly on the test when they're actually very smart. Tests also only look at one day in a student's life instead of how they **perform** in school over a longer amount of time.

Know the Facts!

Students who are still learning English often have to take the same standardized tests as students who've been speaking English for their whole lives.

Even very smart students might have a bad day that causes them to do poorly on a test.

19

Taking tests can be stressful for both teachers and students. However, there are still many reasons why tests are used to measure how smart students are and how good teachers are at their jobs. Although some students might dream of a world without tests, many people believe that's not a good idea.

After learning all the facts about why people support and oppose tests, what do you think? Should students have to take tests? What facts helped shape your point of view?

Should STUDENTS have to take TESTS?

YES

- Tests show how well teachers are doing their jobs and help teachers see if their methods are working.

- Tests help students learn and remember what they've been taught.

- Tests are the most fair and objective way to compare students.

NO

- Teachers feel they need to teach to the tests students take, which stops students from getting a well-rounded education.

- Tests can cause anxiety.

- Tests don't always accurately measure how smart students are.

These are just some of the reasons people support and oppose tests. Can you think of any more?

GLOSSARY

accurate: Free of mistakes.

district: An area set apart for some purpose.

focus: To concentrate attention or effort.

frequent: Happening often.

funding: Money for a special purpose.

human error: A mistake made by a person instead of a machine.

issue: A point of discussion or debate.

perform: To do something that requires a skill.

respond: To have a certain reaction to something.

stress: A state of worry and strain in the mind caused by problems in life.

unit: Part of a school course with a central theme.

For More INFORMATION

WEBSITES

Test Anxiety

kidshealth.org/en/teens/test-anxiety.html
This website gives visitors a better understanding of test anxiety, including what causes it and how to deal with it.

Test Stress: A Fact of Life

pbskids.org/itsmylife/school/teststress
This PBS website features facts about facing test anxiety and a list of reasons why tests are good for students.

BOOKS

Henke, Emma MacLaren, and Stacy Peterson. *School Rules!: Tips, Tricks, Shortcuts, and Secrets to Make You a Super Student.* Middleton, WI: American Girl Publishing, 2016.

Moss, Wendy, and Robin A. DeLuca-Acconi. *School Made Easier: A Kid's Guide to Study Strategies and Anxiety-Busting Tools.* Washington, DC: Magination Press, 2014.

INDEX